09/08

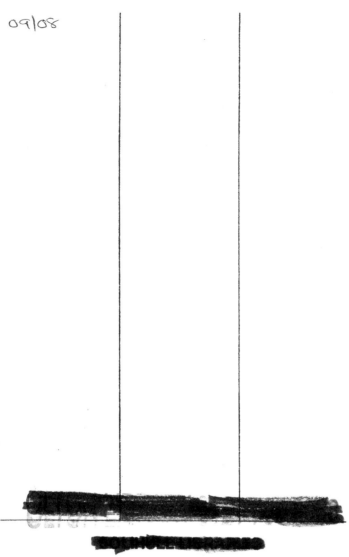

This book must be returned to any Solihull library on or before the latest date stamped on the label. It may be renewed up to three times unless another reader has reserved it.

You may renew by telephoning your local branch during library opening hours.

Details of charges, loan periods and other matters may be seen in the library or visit our website: www.solihull.gov.uk/wwwlib/

BORROWERS are responsible for any damage to items while in their possession.

L.3

D0235616

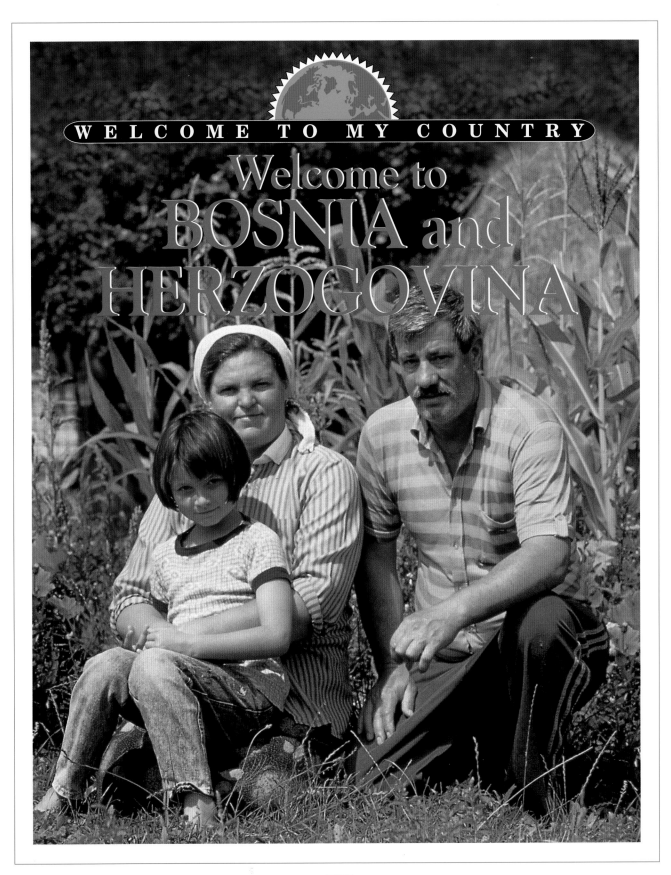

WELCOME TO MY COUNTRY

Welcome to
BOSNIA and
HERZOGOVINA

W
FRANKLIN WATTS
LONDON·SYDNEY

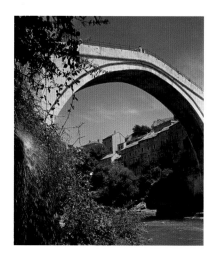

This edition first published in 2005 by
Franklin Watts
96 Leonard Street
London EC2A 4XD

Franklin Watts Australia
45-51 Huntley Street
Alexandria NSW 2015

This edition is published for sale only in the United Kingdom & Eire.

© Marshall Cavendish International (Asia) Pte Ltd 2005
Originated and designed by Times Editions–Marshall Cavendish
an imprint of Marshall Cavendish International (Asia) Pte Ltd
A member of the Times Publishing Group
Times Centre, 1 New Industrial Road
Singapore 536196

Written by: Umaima Mulla-Feroze & Matilda Gabrielpillai
Editor: Melvin Neo
Designer: Geoslyn Lim
Picture researcher: Susan Jane Manuel

A CIP catalogue record for this book
is available from the British Library.

ISBN 0 7496 6010 4

Printed in Singapore

PICTURE CREDITS
ANA. Press Agency: 26 (top), 33, 37
Archive Photos: 15, 16
Art Directors & TRIP Photographic Library:
    2, 4, 8, 14, 17, 18, 19, 23, 24, 25,
    26 (bottom), 27, 31, 35, 40, 41, 43
Robert Bremac: 28, 36, 38, 45
Bruce Coleman Collection: 3 (centre), 9
Evergreen Photo Alliance: Cover, 1, 3 (top),
    20, 21, 22, 29, 32, 34
Focus Team – Italy: 7
Simeon Glumac: 39
The Hutchison Library: 5
North Wind Picture Archives: 10
Topham Picturepoint: 3 (bottom), 6, 12, 13, 30
Vision Photo Agency: 11

Digital Scanning by Superskill Graphics Pte Ltd

Contents

Words that appear in the glossary are printed in **boldface** type the first time they occur in the text.

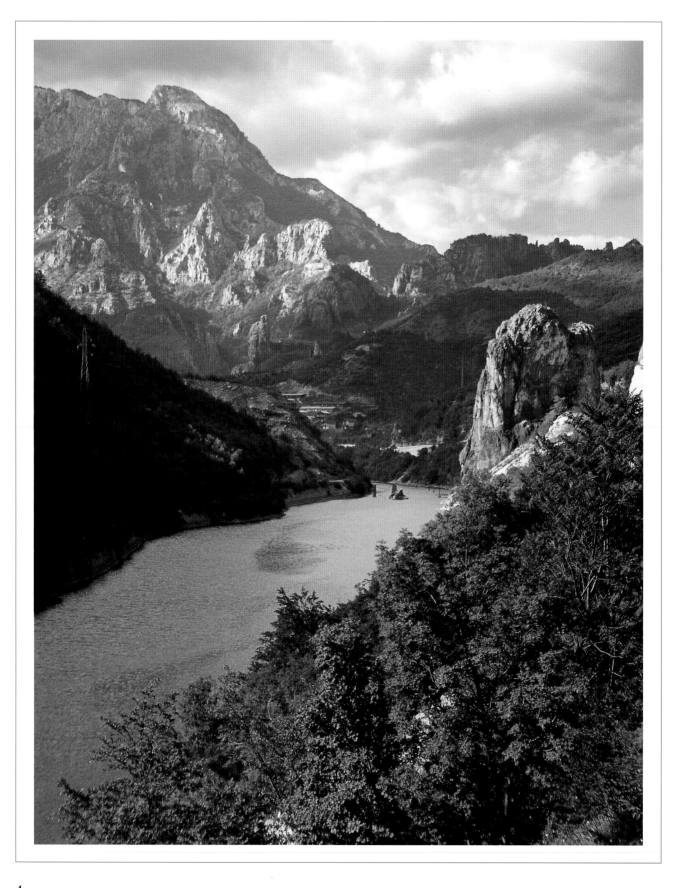

Welcome to Bosnia and Herzegovina!

Bosnia and Herzegovina is sometimes simply called Bosnia, but the country has two **distinct** regions. Bosnia is in the north. Herzegovina is in the south. Let's explore beautiful Bosnia and learn about its history and its people.

Opposite: The Neretva River is just one example of Herzegovina's natural beauty.

Below: Bosnia's capital, Sarajevo, is the country's most **cosmopolitan** city.

The Flag of Bosnia & Herzegovina

The flag adopted in 1998 has a yellow triangle on a blue background. The triangle's points stand for Bosnia's three main **ethnic** groups. The stars represent the Council of Europe. The half stars represent Bosnia's two regions.

The Land

Bosnia has an area of 51,129 square kilometres. It is located on the Balkan **Peninsula** which is the largest European peninsula on the Mediterranean Sea. Serbia and Montenegro border Bosnia on the east and the south-east. Except for a very short south-western coastline on the Adriatic Sea, the rest of the country is surrounded by Croatia. The capital city of Bosnia is Sarajevo.

Below: This steep waterfall on the Vrbas River is near the town of Jajce.

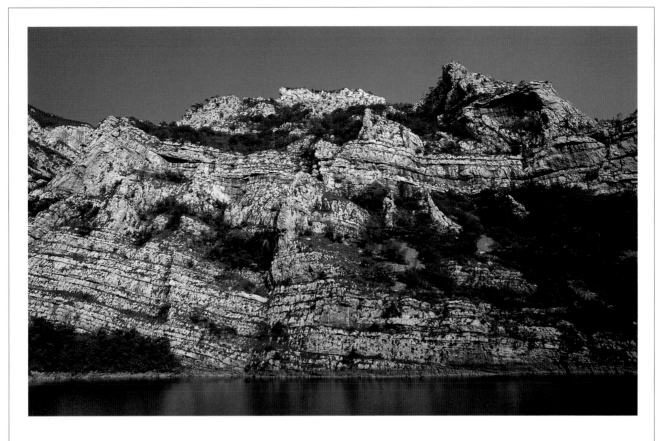

Mountain ranges stretch across southern and western Bosnia, and the Dinaric Alps form a natural western border with Croatia. At 2,386 metres, Mount Maglic on the south-eastern border is Bosnia's highest peak. Herzegovina, Bosnia's southern region, has dry limestone **plateaus** rising as high as 2,000 metres. Bosnia's major rivers are the Bosna, Drina, Sava, Una and Vrbas in the north and the Neretva in the south.

Above:
Magnificent cliffs border the banks of the Neretva River in the southern region of Herzegovina.

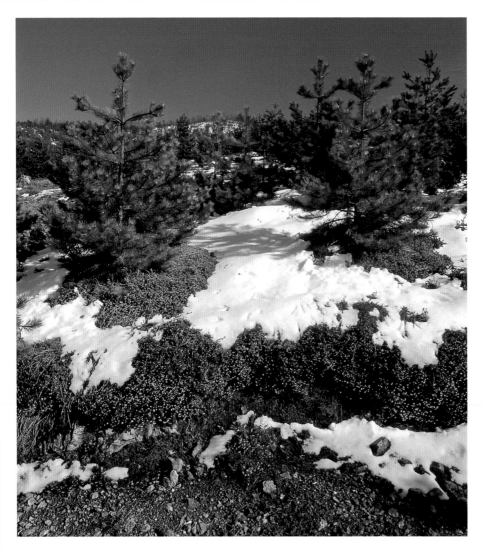

Left: Northern Bosnia gets a lot of snow in winter. Patches of snow are still on the ground even at the end of the season.

Climate

The Dinaric Alps shelter Bosnia from the Adriatic Sea, keeping its climate **moderate**. In the northern city of Banja Luka, temperatures are about 0° Celsius (C) in winter and 22° C in summer. Mostar in the south has temperatures ranging from 6° C to 38° C.

Plants and Animals

Beech, oak and pine forests grow abundantly in Bosnia's fertile northern region. Even the dry southern region of Herzegovina has areas where fig and cypress trees thrive.

Bosnia's wildlife includes animals such as wolves, wildcats, otters, falcons, foxes and Herzegovinian bears.

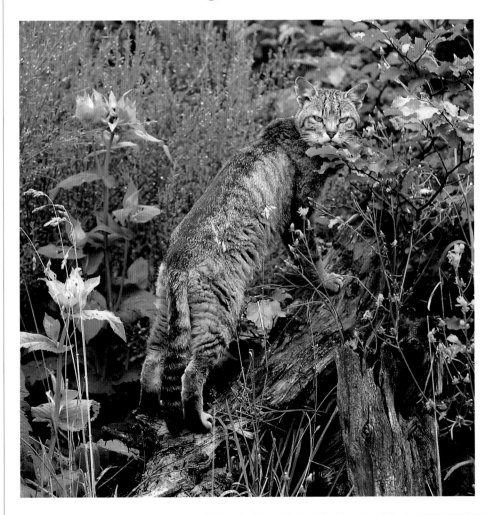

Left: The European wildcat is normally a shy animal, but it can be fierce when it is scared or if it feels threatened.

History

The Illyrians were the first people known to settle in the area that is now Bosnia. The Romans conquered most of Bosnia in the first century A.D., and the powerful Serbs and Croats from Central Europe ruled from the seventh to the twelfth century.

From 1180 to 1463, Hungary controlled Bosnia and the country was governed by **viceroys** called *bans*. Ban Stjepan Kotromanic, who reigned from

Left: The Illyrians were settled in the western part of the Balkan Peninsula by the seventh century B.C.

10

1322 to 1353, conquered Herzegovina (then called Hum), uniting the two regions until Herzegovina broke away in 1448.

The Turks captured Bosnia in 1463 and Herzegovina in 1483, making both regions provinces of the Ottoman Empire. Peasant unrest in 1875 and war with Russia in 1877 led international powers to decide that the Austro-Hungarian Empire should take over in Bosnia.

The Rise and Fall of Yugoslavia

Austria-Hungary **annexed** Bosnia in 1908 because Serbia and Croatia wanted to control Bosnia and establish the independent state of Yugoslavia. In 1914, Gavrilo Princip, a Bosnian Serb, killed the heir to the Austro-Hungarian throne. Austria-Hungary responded by declaring war on Serbia, and this started World War I.

When the war ended in 1918, the Austro-Hungarian Empire broke apart. Bosnia became part of the Kingdom of Serbs, Croats and Slovenes, which was renamed Yugoslavia in 1929.

In the 1940s during World War II, Germany occupied part of Yugoslavia, including Bosnia. Josip Broz Tito, a Croatian, led a **resistance movement** that freed Bosnia from the Germans in 1945. Bosnia then became part of a communist-ruled Yugoslav federation, which also included Croatia, Serbia, Herzegovina, Montenegro, Slovenia, Kosovo, Vojvodina and Macedonia. Tito was its president. When Tito died in 1980, the federation fell apart.

Below: General Josip Broz Tito reviews Yugoslav soldiers in 1944. The Yugoslav army was powerful, even after Tito's death.

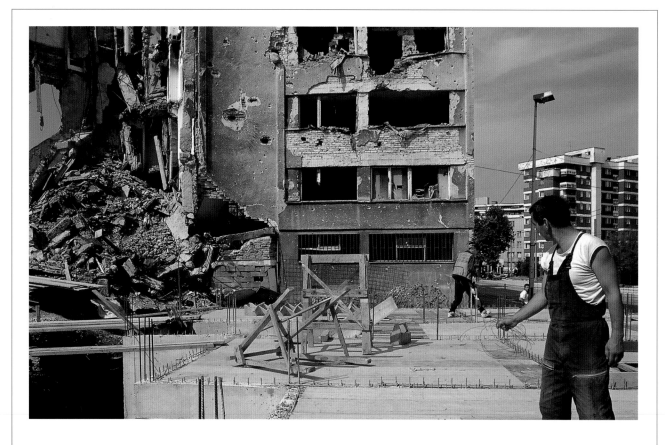

The Ethnic War of 1992–1995

In 1992, Bosnia and Herzegovina claimed independence but a horrible ethnic war followed. Serbs wanted to reunite all of the Yugoslav territories but **eliminate** all non-Serbian people. The Serbian army attacked Sarajevo and other Bosnian towns, **persecuting** or killing non-Serbs. Peace talks in 1995 divided Bosnia into the Serb Republika Srpska and the Federation of Bosnia and Herzegovina.

Above: Much of Sarajevo had to be rebuilt after the war of 1992–1995.

Ban Kulin (r. 1180–1204)

Although *ban* is a title normally given by Hungarian kings, Ban Kulin took it for himself. During his reign, he freed Bosnia from Hungary, expanded its territory and brought peace and prosperity to the land.

King Tvrtko I (1338–1391)

Bosnia's first king and greatest ruler, Tvrtko I, made his country the most powerful state in the Balkans. Conquests made during his reign increased Bosnia's land. By 1390, Bosnia included parts of Croatia, Slovenia and Montenegro.

Alija Izetbegovic (1925–2003)

A member of the Muslim Party of Democratic Action, Alija Izetbegovic was elected President of Bosnia in 1990. With the leaders of Serbia and Croatia, he signed the peace agreement that ended the ethnic war of 1992–1995.

Alija Izetbegovic

Government and the Economy

The current system of government in Bosnia was established by the 1995 peace agreement that divided the country into the Serbian Republic, or Republika Srpska, and the Federation of Bosnia and Herzegovina. Both the Republic and the Federation each have a local president and a **parliament**.

Below:
A conference on Bosnia in 1998 brought together leaders of more than fifty countries. The members of Bosnia's **tripartite** presidency who attended were Croat Ante Jelavic (*left*), Serb Zivko Radisic (*centre*) and Bosniak Alija Izetbegovic (*right*).

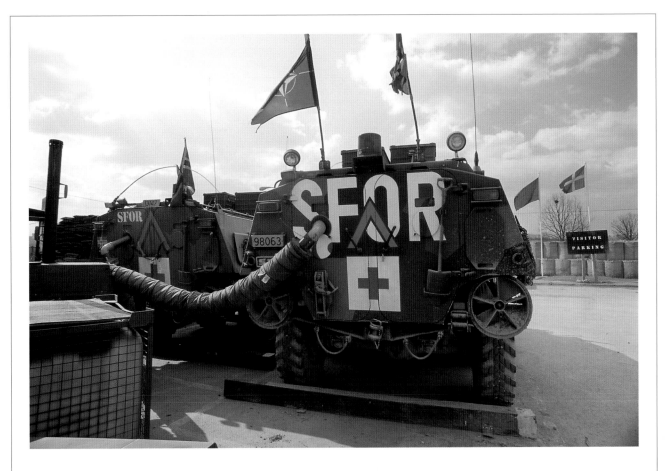

The central government has three presidents, one elected from each of the three main ethnic groups — Serbs, Bosniaks and Croats. This tripartite presidency appoints a Council of Ministers in charge of foreign policy, trade and other national issues.

The United Nations, the United States of America and the European Union all played a role in Bosnia's peace talks and are active in its government.

Above:
Peacekeeping is an international effort in Bosnia. The Stabilisation Force (SFOR) is made up of troops from more than thirty nations.

The Economy

The war of 1992–1995 destroyed Bosnia's economy. Industries stopped producing and many people lost their jobs. Since 1995, the country has been reconstructing cities, power lines and telecommunication and transportation systems. More people have jobs again, but 40 per cent are still unemployed.

Left:
One of Bosnia's successes after the war of 1992–1995 was to establish a single, central bank. The Central Bank building is in Sarajevo.

Left: This covered market in Sarajevo sells a variety of food products. Even more products will become available as the government continues to rebuild Bosnia's economy.

Before the war, agriculture and Bosnia's rich mineral resources such as **bauxite**, iron, coal and zinc, contributed more than half of the country's wealth. Today, education, transportation, banking and health care services are more important.

In 1998, Bosnia introduced major banking and finance **reforms** and established a national currency, the convertible mark. Bosnia still needs international aid and loans. With a recovering economy, however, it will need less foreign aid in the future.

People and Lifestyle

The people of Bosnia belong to many ethnic groups, but almost all of them are **descendants** of the South Slav people who settled in the western Balkans in the seventh century. The three main ethnic groups are Serbs, Bosniaks and Croats.

Minority groups in Bosnia include the Romany, who are descendants of **nomadic** people from India, and Jews. Together these minorities form less than 1 per cent of Bosnia's population.

Below: Home for this Bosniak family is a village close to the city of Sarajevo.

Left: Sarajevo has a youth club that is open to Bosnian children of all ethnic groups. At this club, children learn, through art, how to deal with the **trauma** of war.

Serbs, Bosniaks and Croats

Ethnic identity is very important to Bosnians. Approximately 37 per cent of the population is Serb, 48 per cent is Bosniak and 14 per cent is Croat. After the war of 1992–1995, Bosnia was divided into two regions. Serbs occupy the region known today as Republika Srpska. The Bosniaks and the Croats live in the Federation of Bosnia and Herzegovina. Very few areas have a mixture of ethnic groups.

Family Life

The home and family are the heart of Bosnian life, but the war destroyed Bosnian homes and separated family members. Some have still not found their loved ones. For those who survived the war, life now revolves around providing a better future for their children.

Left:
Family values have a strong influence on social activities in Bosnia. Family members spend a lot of time together.

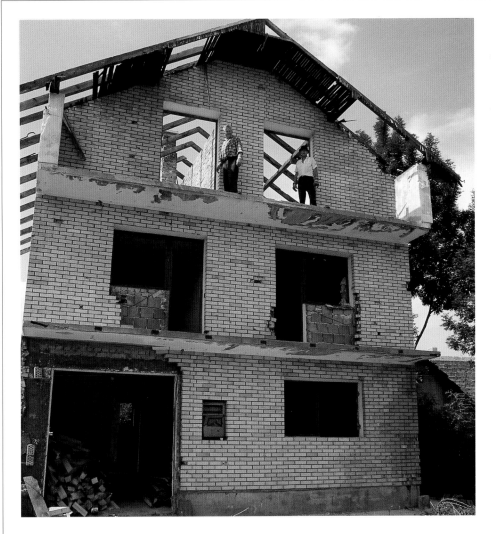

Left: Life in Bosnia is slowly returning to normal as people rebuild their homes and their lives after the war.

Some survivors of the war had to rebuild their homes. Others had to rebuild their lives. Forced out of their homes, towns and villages, they had to find new safe communities with members of their own ethnic group. Many moved from country villages to find work in the cities. Yet, be it in the city or country, family ties remain strong.

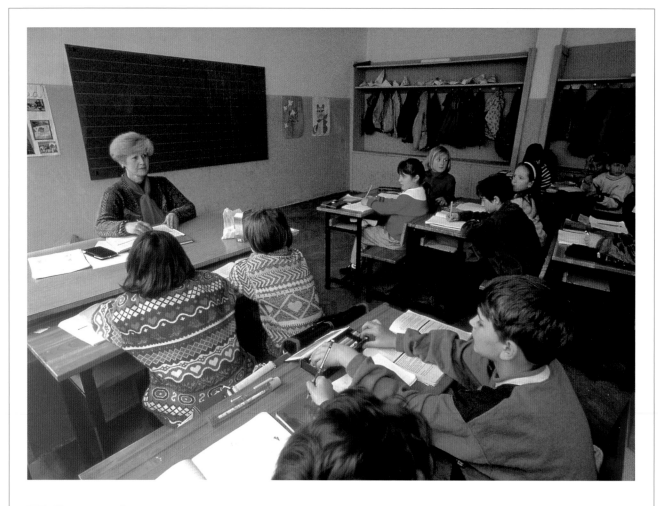

Education

When Bosnia was in the Yugoslav federation, **illiteracy**, especially among women and in rural areas, was high. Steps taken in the 1990s to improve the country's education system suffered a setback when schools became targets in the war of 1992–1995. Today, schools are being repaired or rebuilt.

Above: Most of the children in Bosnia start school at the age of seven. All Bosnian children must attend primary school.

In Bosnia, children attend eight years of primary school and four years of secondary school. Many also attend religious classes held at a **mosque** or a church.

Bosnia has four universities. The University of Sarajevo, built in 1949, is the oldest and largest. The others are in Mostar, Tuzla and Banja Luka.

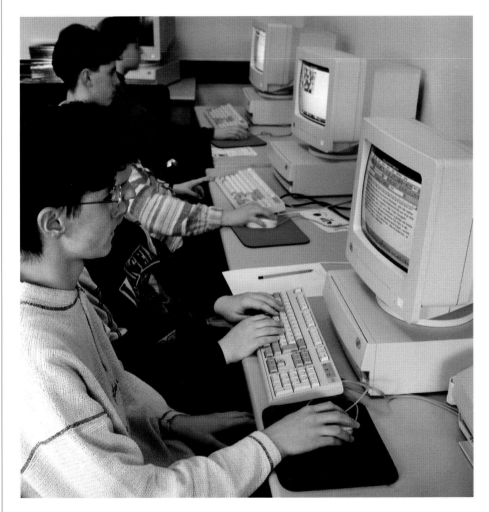

Left: Some of the secondary schools in Bosnia have computer facilities for their students. This computer room is at a school in Sarajevo.

Religion

Bosnia's constitution gives citizens the freedom to practise any religion. In reality, however, people can safely practice a faith only where that faith is the main religion.

Bosnia has three main religions, and religion and ethnic identity are closely related. Serbs are usually Eastern Orthodox Christians. Most Bosniaks are Muslims. Croats are usually Roman Catholics. A small number of Bosnians are Jews or Protestants or belong to other faiths.

Above: Catholics living in Sarajevo attend the Cathedral of Jesus' Heart.

Left: These Muslim men are reading the Qur'an, the Islamic holy book, at a mosque in Mostar. Islam has many followers in Bosnia.

During communist rule, religion was discouraged in Bosnia. Today, young Bosnians, especially the Croats in Herzegovina, seem to be returning to religion. Among Muslim Bosniaks, however, most do not strictly follow Islamic rules. Bosniak women for example, do not wear veils.

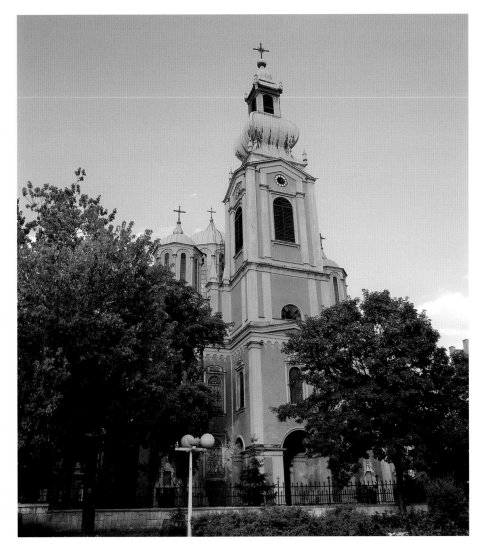

Left: The design of a Serb Orthodox church, such as this one in Sarajevo, is similar to other Eastern Orthodox churches. The inside is usually decorated with scenes from the Bible such as the Last Supper.

Language

Bosnians have one common language, Serbo-Croatian. It has been used since the twelfth century. During Ottoman rule, however, about 6,000 Turkish words found their way into this South Slav language.

Today, Bosniaks call the language Bosnian, Croats call it Croatian and Serbs call it Serbian. Bosniaks and Croats write the language in Roman script. Serbs use Cyrillic script. Any educated Bosnian can read both scripts.

Left: This sign reads "Welcome to Republic of Srpska" in Cyrillic script. This script was invented in the ninth century by a Greek monk named Cyril.

Left: Books that were rescued from stores destroyed in the war of 1992–1995 are now showing up in book stalls on the streets of Sarajevo.

Literature

Bosnia's literature reflects a mixture of cultures including Slav, Turkish, Greek, Arabic and European. For example, a form of Bosnian poetry called Aljamiado literature has Arab and Spanish influences.

Folk poetry is one of the country's most important literary forms. The sad love poem *Hasanaganica*, or *The Wife of Hasan Aga*, became one of the most popular folk poems in Europe. It was translated by famous European writers, such as Lord Byron of England, into their own languages.

Arts

Architecture

The buildings in Bosnia combine Islamic, European, Roman, Gothic and other similar architectural styles. Many buildings were damaged or destroyed in the war of 1992–1995. In restoring and rebuilding them, Bosnians are trying to preserve their architectural **heritage**.

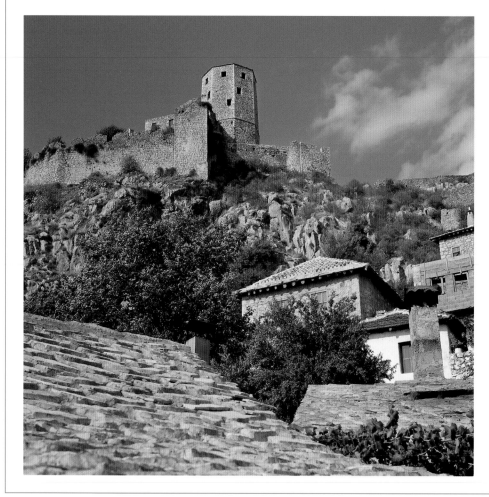

Left: One of the remaining stone fortresses built by the Ottoman Turks overlooks a town in Herzegovina.

Bosnia still has some of the spectacular mosques and impressive stone fortresses built by the Ottoman Turks. Ottoman architecture often had Christian elements such as tall, narrow, stained-glass windows.

Mosques throughout the country also have beautifully carved wooden staircases. Wood carving is an ancient craft in Bosnia. Traditionally, houses were built almost entirely of wood and furniture was elaborately carved.

Above: This house in Mostar was built in the seventeenth century. Its **ornate** wooden furniture is elaborately carved with geometric and floral designs.

Traditional Crafts

During Turkish rule, many Bosnian craftspeople were skilled in the arts of calligraphy, miniature painting, manuscript **illumination** and leather bookbinding, which were all part of producing books. Bookbinding is still a strong tradition in Sarajevo.

Carpet weaving is another ancient craft. The Persians, who were master carpet weavers, were responsible for developing this art in Bosnia. Today, the carpets produced in each different town have their own unique design.

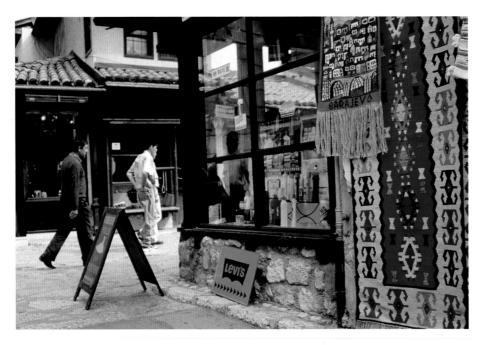

Left: A beautifully designed Bosnian carpet hangs outside a shop in Mostar. Other centres of carpet manufacturing in Bosnia are the cities of Foča, Stolac, Gacko, Visegrad and Sarajevo.

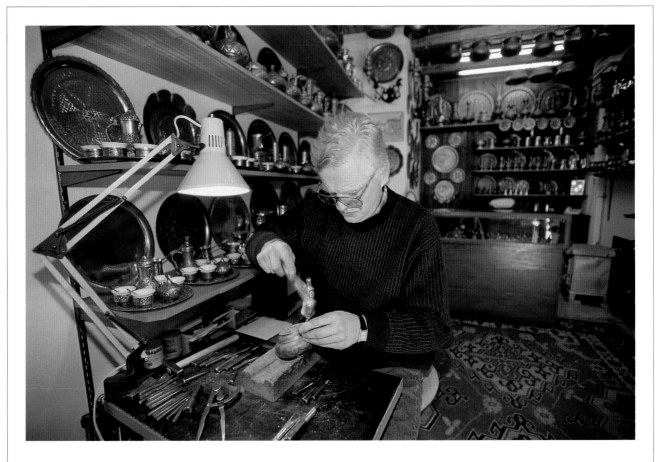

Elegant fabrics and embroidered pillowcases and cushion covers are also part of Bosnia's artistic tradition. Textile manufacturing is a leading industry, producing valuable fabrics such as velvet and brocade.

Bosnia is also well known for its metalwork. Techniques such as **engraving**, **embossing**, **encrustation** and **filigree** are used in decorating metal jewellery and household utensils.

Above:
This craftsman is embossing a metal container at his studio in Sarajevo. Metalworkers in Sarajevo specialise in embossing and engraving. Banja Luka has the best filigree workers.

Leisure

Bosnians are warm friendly people. In rural villages, neighbours often visit each other just to chat. These visits are called *ide na kafu* or coffee visits. Village women often meet to exchange news. Special events, such as weddings, birthdays and homecomings, are also occasions for visiting. Rural Bosnians entertain each other by telling stories.

Left: Leisure time in rural areas of Bosnia is often spent enjoying coffee with family and friends.

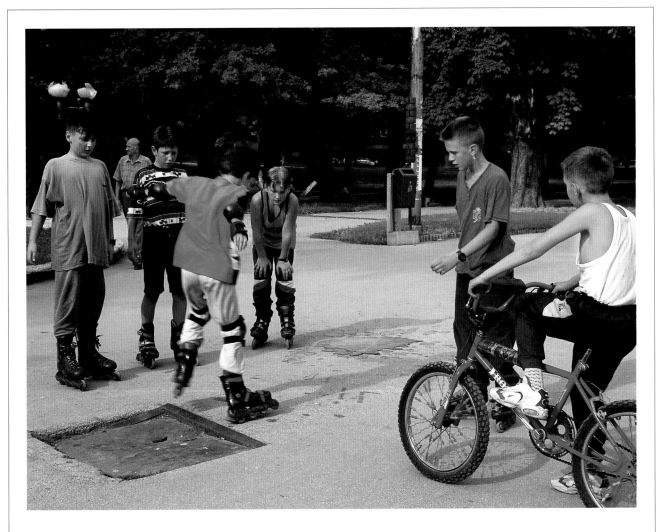

Embroidery is another popular pastime for rural women. Many ethnic groups can be identified by the distinct patterns of embroidery on their clothes.

Urban Bosnians also enjoy spending time with family and friends. They like to go shopping, meet at a café, go to the cinema or walk in the park. Reading and embroidery are popular indoor activities.

Above: In Bosnian cities, in-line skating and riding bicycles are popular outdoor activities.

Sports

The mountains, rivers and wildlife in Bosnia have helped determine some of the country's favourite sports and outdoor activities. In winter, Bosnians go cross-country skiing, ice-skating and sledging. Children in the cities even sledge down snow-covered streets.

Hunting is a major sport in early summer and the huge Herzegovinian brown bear is a special challenge for hunters. This plant-eating bear is so strong it can uproot trees.

Bosnia's lakes Jablanicko Jezero and Busko Jezero are known as the best fishing spots in the region. The country's rocky mountain ranges and thick forests are a challenge for hikers.

The most popular team sports in Bosnia are football and basketball. The country has three football leagues and two basketball leagues. The national football team took fourth place in its group during the qualifying round for the Euro 2000 football championships.

Below: Bosnian teenagers often get together for neighbourhood football games, especially in the summertime.

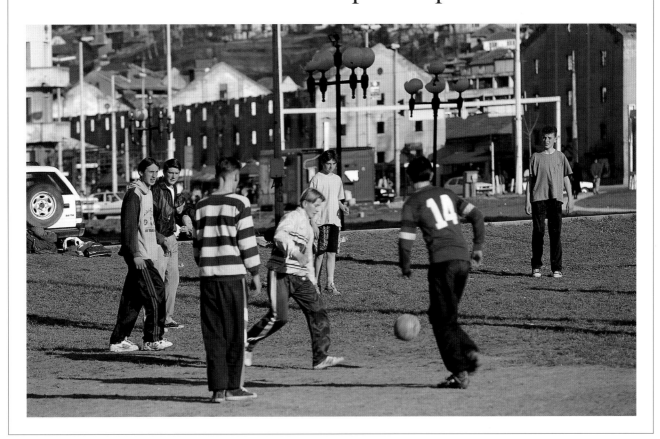

Festivals

With three major religions, Bosnians celebrate many religious festivals. They also participate in festivals that are not part of any particular religion.

Bajram is a three-day Muslim festival celebrated immediately after Ramadan, the Muslim month of **fasting**. Muslims also celebrate the anniversaries of their mosques.

Left: Strings of colourful electric lights decorate the Gazi Husrev-Bey mosque in Sarajevo during the Muslim festival of Bajram.

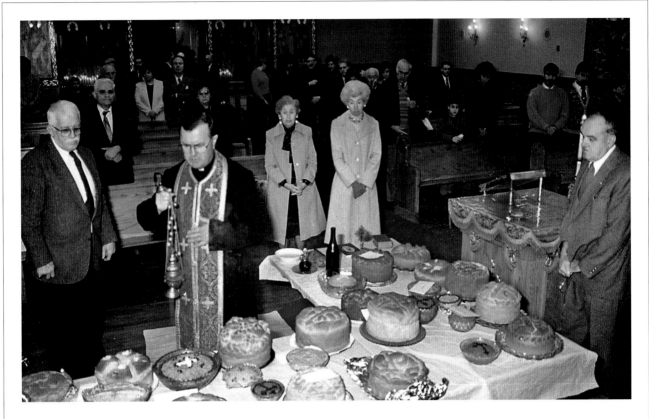

Krsna Slava honours the spiritual birthday of the Serbian people. Each family holds this festival on the day their family or tribe was first baptised into the Eastern Orthodox Church.

Above: Families celebrate Krsna Slava at an Eastern Orthodox church. Bread prepared as an offering to thank God for his blessings is part of the ceremony.

More than half of all Bosnians celebrate Christmas but all regions do not celebrate the same way. Serbs decorate a *badnjak,* or Christmas tree, with ribbons, fruits, nuts and candies. They also put straw under it to symbolise Christ's manger.

Food

Bosnian cooking combines the flavours of the Mediterranean, Central Europe, the Balkans and the Middle East.

Cevapcici is seasoned lamb, pork or beef sausage that is grilled with onions and served on thick pitta bread. *Bosanski lonac* is Bosnian hotpot stew. It is a delicious mixture of slowly roasted meat and vegetables served in a cooking pot.

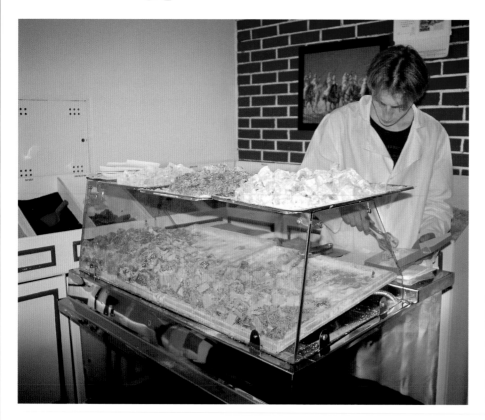

Left: Bosnians eat an assortment of sweets including Turkish delight. This sweet comes in many different flavours, with or without nuts.

The Ottoman Turks introduced stuffed vegetables. Ground meat, rice, spices and chopped vegetables are wrapped in cabbage leaves or stuffed inside hollowed-out peppers, potatoes or onions, and cooked slowly in a tightly covered dish over an open fire.

Baklava is a popular pastry dessert with a sweet filling of chopped nuts and honey.

Above: This market in Sarajevo offers a variety of fruits including grapes, apples, plums, pomegranates and pears. Bosnia is known for its "Turkish plums" called damsons.

A   **B**   **C**   **D**

SLOVENIA

HUNGARY

BOSNIA AND HERZEGOVINA

1

Sava

Sava

Danube

Vojvodina

2

Una

● Banja Luka

Bosna

Sava

BELGRADE ●

Vrbas

B O S N I A (region)

Tuzla ●

● Jajce

Bosna

Bosna

Drina

Serbia

CROATIA

A

YUGOSLAVIA

3

R

SARAJEVO ■

Visegrad ●

Busko
Jezero

Jablanicko
Jezero

HERZEGOVINA
(region)

Foča ●

Neretva

Mostar ●

● Stolac

Gacko ●

▲ Mount Maglic
(2,386 metres)

4

A

M o n t e n e g r o

Kosovo

L

P

S

N

ADRIATIC SEA

5

ALBANIA

———	State Boundary
- - - -	Regional Boundary
———	Entity Boundary
▨	Republika Srpska
▨	Federation of Bosnia and Herzegovina
■	Capital
●	City
∿	River

Dalmatian coast

42

Above: The Old Town area of Sarajevo is a historic part of the city.

Adriatic Sea A3–C5
Albania D5

Banja Luka B2
Belgrade
 (Serbia) D2
Bosna River C2–C3
Bosnia (region)
 A2–C4
Busko Jezero
 (lake) B3

Croatia A1–C5

Dalmatian Coast
 A3–C4
Danube River
 C1–D2
Dinaric Alps A2–D5
Drina River D2–C4

Federation of
 Bosnia and
 Herzegovina
 A2–C4
Foča C3

Gacko C4

Herzegovina
 (region) B3–C4
Hungary B1–C1

Jablanicko Jezero
 (lake) B3
Jajce B3

Kosovo D4–D5

Montenegro C4–D5
Mostar B4
Mount Maglic C4

Neretva River
 B4–C4
Republika Srpska
 A2–C4

Sarajevo C3
Sava River A1–D2
Serbia D2–D4
Slovenia A1

Stolac B4

Tuzla C2

Una River A3–B2

Visegrad D3
Vojvodina C1-D2
Vrbas River B2–B3

Yugoslavia C1–D5

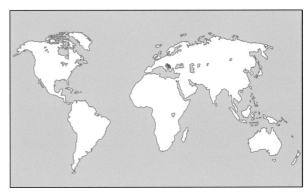

Quick Facts

Official Name	Bosnia and Herzegovina
Capital	Sarajevo
Official Language	Serbo-Croatian (Bosnian, Croatian or Serbian)
Population	4,007,608 (July 2004 estimate)
Land Area	51,129 square kilometres
Administrative Divisions	Federation of Bosnia and Herzegovina, Republika Srpska
Highest Point	Mount Maglic (2,386 metres)
Major Rivers	Bosna, Drina, Neretva, Sava, Una, Vrbas
Main Religions	Eastern Orthodox Christianity, Islam, Roman Catholicism
Main Ethnic Groups	Bosniaks, Croats, Serbs
Currency	Convertible Mark (2.942 BAM = £1 as at July 2004)

Opposite: The town of Jajce rises above this beautiful waterfall on the Vrbas River.

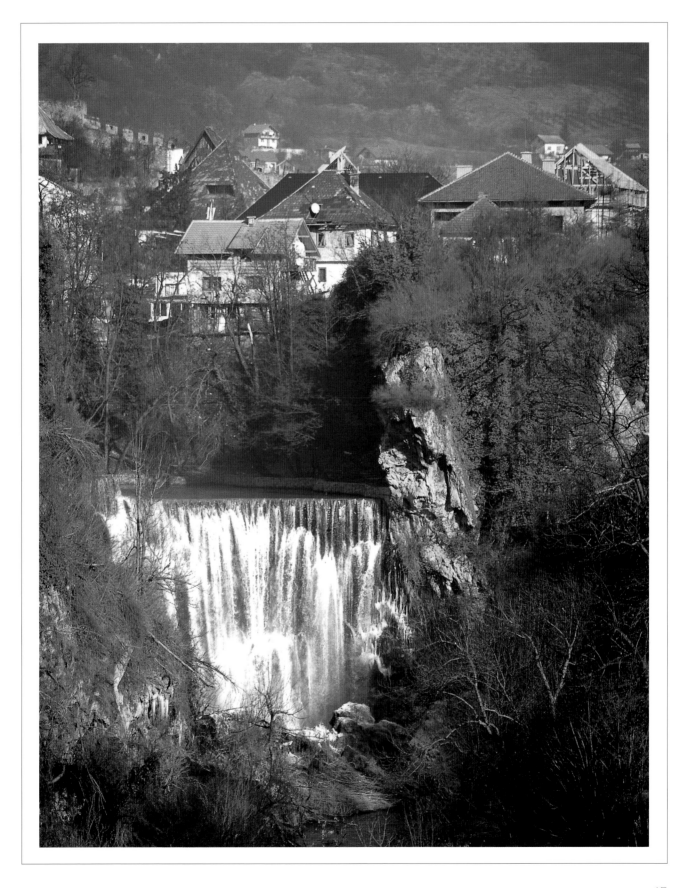

Glossary

annexed: added a country or territory to the existing territory of the controlling country or state.

assassin: a person who kills someone, often for political or religious reasons.

bauxite: the material from which aluminium is made.

cosmopolitan: having an international appearance and worldwide appeal.

descendants: the line of people born within a certain family or culture of ancestors.

distinct: different in a noticeable way.

eliminate: get rid of.

embossing: decorating with a design that is raised above the surface.

encrustation: the design technique of filling in carvings with silver, gold or pearl.

engraving: lightly carving figures or designs into a solid surface.

ethnic: related to a certain race or culture of people.

fasting: not eating food for a certain period of time.

filigree: the art of making delicate designs by twisting fine wire.

heritage: the styles and practices passed down by earlier generations.

illiteracy: the inability to read or write due to a lack of education.

illumination: the art of decorating books or manuscripts with silver, gold or brilliant colours and designs.

moderate: not extreme.

mosque: a place where Muslims go to pray.

nomadic: wandering or moving around without having a permanent home.

ornate: having a lot of decoration.

parliament: a group of elected government representatives who make the laws for their country.

peninsula: a long piece of land that is surrounded by water on three sides.

persecuting: treating cruelly, and often torturing, because of race, religion, culture or political beliefs.

plateaus: large areas of high, flat land that rise sharply above the land around them.

reforms: changes or improvements, usually to correct problems.

resistance movement: an organised effort to oppose and change an existing government.

trauma: severe emotional shock.

tripartite: made up of three parties.

viceroys: people who govern a province or a colony as a representative of the ruler of another country.

More Books to Read

Assassination in Sarajevo. Days That Shook the World series. Alex Woolf (Hodder Wayland)

Assassination in Sarajevo. Turning Points in History series. Stewart Ross (Heinemann Library)

The Balkans. Flashpoints series. Simon Adams (Franklin Watts)

Mirad, a Boy from Bosnia. New Century Readers. Ad de Bont (Longman)

The Ottoman Empire: 1450-1700. Access to History series. Andrina Stiles (Hodder Arnold)

War in Yugoslavia. Headliners series. Edward R. Ricciuti (Evans Brothers)

Web Sites

news.bbc.co.uk/hi/english/static/map/yugoslavia/

www.megastories.com/bosnia/history/history.htm

www.oxfam.org.uk/coolplanet/kidsweb/world/Bosnia/.htm

www.serbiapost.com/s/serbiapost/reports_timeline.html

Due to the dynamic nature of the Internet, some web sites stay current longer than others. To find additional web sites, use a reliable search engine with one or more of the following keywords to help you locate information about Bosnia. Keywords: *Balkans, Bosnia, Croatia, Alija Izetbegovic, Mostar, Serbia, Sarajevo.*

Note to parents and teachers
Every effort has been made by the Publishers to ensure that these web sites are suitable for children, that they are of the highest educational value, and that they contain no inappropriate or offensive material. However, because of the nature of the Internet, it is impossible to guarantee that the contents of these sites will not be altered. We strongly advise that Internet access is supervised by a responsible adult.

Index